A New True Book

AUTOMOBILES

By Sylvia Wilkinson

*This "true book" was prepared
under the direction of
Illa Podendorf,
formerly with the Laboratory School,
University of Chicago*

CHILDRENS PRESS, CHICAGO

PHOTO CREDITS

Hay Hillstrom—2, 13 (top right), 14 (top)

Root Associates—© Mary Root, 42, Earl L. Kubis, Cover

NASA—22

Art Thoma Photo—4 (2 photos), 13 (top left)

Jan Bigelow—35

Candee & Associates—14 (bottom), 17 (top)

Ford Motor Company—6, 7

Tony Freeman—37

Joseph A. DiChello, Jr.—8, 13 (middle left), 20 (right), 23, 27, 44

Wayne Hartman—19

National Highway Traffic Safety Administration— 10, 11 (2 photos), 25, 38 (2 photos)

James Rowan—13 (bottom left)

Reinhard Brucker—13 (middle right), 20 (left), 40

John Forsberg—28-29, 31, 32, 34

Wayne Hartman—17 (bottom)

COVER—Driving an antique car

Library of Congress Cataloging in Publication Data

Wilkinson, Sylvia, 1940-
  Automobiles.

  (A New true book)
  Includes index.
  Summary: Describes different types of automobiles and their purposes and discusses automobile design and other related topics such as gasoline, mileage, and safety.
  1. Automobiles—Juvenile literature.
[1. Automobiles]   I. Title.
TL147.W53   629.2'222   82-4441
ISBN 0-516-01608-3   AACR2

TABLE OF CONTENTS

EARLY AUTOMOBILES

Once people had to walk everywhere they wanted to go. Then people tamed animals.

Horses, camels, oxen, and llamas became work animals. They carried people and things on their backs. They pulled wagons and carriages. In many places animals are still used to do this work.

Norman Rockwell's painting shows Henry Ford working on his first car, The Quadricycle, in 1896.

Then inventors made a new kind of carriage. It had an engine to make it go. It was called a horseless carriage or automobile. We also call it a car.

Norman Rockwell painting showing early car scaring horses.

At first many people thought cars were a bad thing. They scared the horses. The cars got stuck in the mud. They broke down.

But soon, people learned to build them better. The automobile was an important invention. It changed the world.

ALL KINDS
OF AUTOMOBILES

Many different kinds of horseless carriages are made.

Trucks, buses, vans, and pickup trucks are horseless carriages. They are built to do or carry special things.

Early cars often got stuck on muddy roads.

Most automobiles are
built to carry people. They
are called passenger cars.
Here are some of the
very first cars ever built.
Not many people drove
cars then.

Soon more and more people drove cars. The people who built cars found many uses for them.

Cars are useful. But cars can cause trouble. Too many cars cause traffic jams. The gases caused by cars that run on gasoline have made the air dirty.

These cars show
how automobile
design has changed
over the years.

Sports cars have always been popular.

SPECIAL CARS TODAY

Sports cars are very small cars. They usually have seats for only two people. Sports cars are fast. They are fun to drive.

Station wagons are big cars. They can carry many things.

Luxury cars are very comfortable. They have lots of room. Some luxury cars are called limousines, or limos.

Race cars are very special cars. They are built to go fast on special race tracks.

Above: Rolls Royce   Below: Lola T530 race car

THE BEETLE

In the early 1950s a
very small car was brought
to the United States from
Germany. Many people
laughed at it because it
was funny looking.

It looked like a bug. In
fact, it was called a
Beetle—a Volkswagen
Beetle. This little car

Volkswagen Beetle

changed everything. It was
not beautiful, but it was
wonderful. It was meant to
use very little gasoline. A
Beetle got thirty-five miles
on one gallon of gas.

Above: Plymouth Duster
Right: Honda Civic

Today the best-selling
automobiles are small.
They burn less gasoline.
They are called compact
cars. They are the cars of
the future.

AIR

Did you know that a car has to push air out of its way? This takes a lot of energy.

People who design cars try to give them shapes that will go easily through the air. They put curves on the fenders. Everything on a car is curved. This makes it easier for the car to move through the air.

When men landed on
the moon, they drove a
special moon car. It was
very different driving
across the moon because
there was no air on the
moon. The moon car didn't
have to be round in shape.

GASOLINE

Most cars run on gasoline. Gasoline is called a fossil fuel. This means it comes from plants and animals that died a long time ago. Fossil fuels are found deep in the ground.

Oil is a fossil fuel. Refineries change the oil into gasoline. They make a different kind of oil to keep the inside of the engine cool. They make grease to keep the parts outside the engine moving smoothly.

Today we are looking for other fuels to run our cars. Did you know that trees, corn, and potatoes can be used to make fuel?

One car runs on energy from the sun. This is a solar car. Another car uses natural gas to make it run. A few cars have been built that run on batteries.

This car is special. It was built for safety. Its tires cannot go flat. It has a strong frame and air bags that inflate to protect riders should the car be in an accident.

GAS MILEAGE

Gas mileage is how many miles a car can go on one gallon of gas. Cars get more miles per gallon on the highway than they do in the city. Do you know why?

In the city the driver must stop the car many times. There are stoplights

and stop signs. Each time
the driver makes the car
move again, the engine
uses more gas.

On the highway the
driver does not stop as
much. So less gas is used.

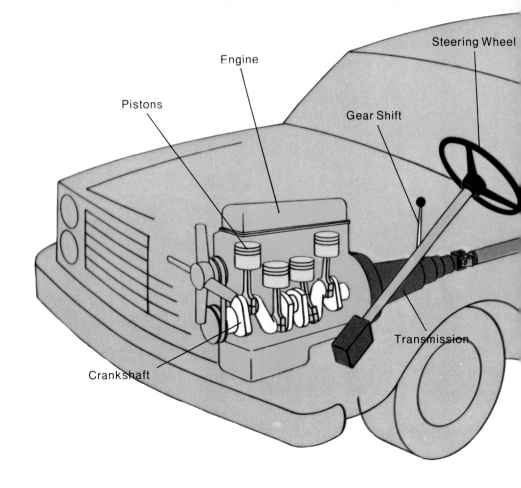

HOW A CAR WORKS

Let's look at what happens inside the car's engine when the driver presses the gas pedal.

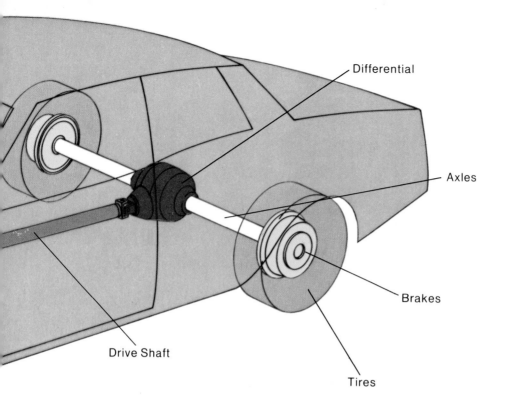

Differential

Axles

Brakes

Drive Shaft

Tires

An engine has cylinders inside it. Some engines have four, some have six, and some have eight. An engine makes power in each cylinder.

To make power an engine needs fuel. It needs air to mix with the fuel so it can burn. And it needs something to make the fuel burn.

The carburetor mixes the fuel with air. This makes vapor, a kind of mist. Then it sends a little of this

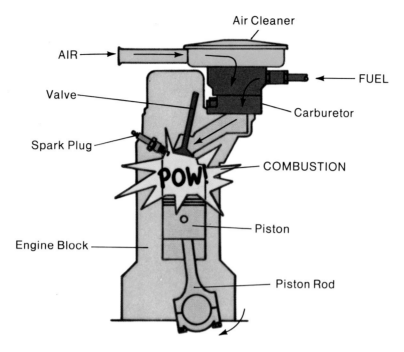

Air Cleaner

AIR →

Valve

Spark Plug

Engine Block

← FUEL

Carburetor

COMBUSTION

Piston

Piston Rod

POW!

vapor into each cylinder. A spark plug makes a spark. Pow! The vapor explodes inside the cylinder. This is combustion.

The explosion pushes a piston down inside the cylinder.

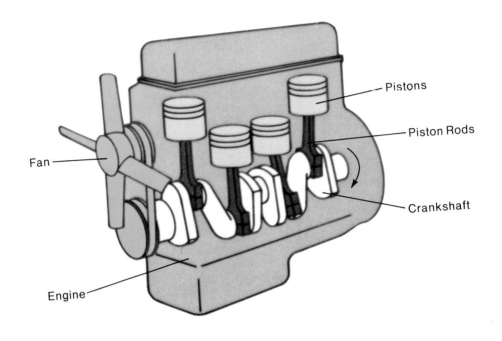

Pistons

Piston Rods

Crankshaft

Fan

Engine

The piston is connected
by a rod to the crankshaft.
When the piston moves
down, the crankshaft turns.
Then the engine is ready
to go to work.

When the driver wants the car to move, he puts it in gear. A gear is a wheel with teeth on it.

The crankshaft turns a gear. This gear turns another gear. This gear turns the drive shaft. These gears hook together as they turn.

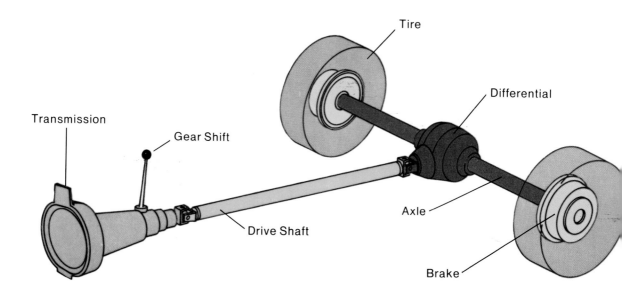

Transmission

Gear Shift

Tire

Differential

Drive Shaft

Axle

Brake

The drive shaft turns the axles with the power given to it by the crankshaft. The axles turn the wheels. When the wheels go around, the car moves.

AUTOMOBILE SAFETY

People need automobiles very much. Many people must drive to work. Many students ride school buses.

But cars can be dangerous. People do get hurt in cars.

Drivers must be careful when they drive cars. Passengers must be careful, too.

The most important way a passenger can make a car safer is to wear a seat belt. Race car drivers always buckle their belts.

Without a seat belt the passenger can hit the dashboard or go through

the glass. Everything in a
car can be dangerous if
the driver hits something.
A seat belt keeps this
from happening.

Every new automobile must be crash tested. The engineers who design cars take them to be tested. They put dummies into each car. They send the cars crashing into walls at different speeds. The dummies show how crashes at different speeds will harm real people. Tests show that in a crash people are always safer if they wear seat belts.

TIRES

Tires are also important
to safety. The first cars
had solid wood wheels.
These were very hard and
gave bumpy rides. Then

rubber was invented. Tires were made of solid rubber. These also gave a bumpy ride. An inner tube filled with air was put inside a hollow tire. The ride got much smoother.

But rubber tires have a problem. If you run over a sharp object, such as a nail, it can put a hole in the tire. This lets out the air and the tire goes flat.

When a rubber tire gets
old and worn, it can split.
If this happens when the
car is moving, it is called
a blowout.

Today many tires have steel threads in them. They cannot blow out like older tires do. They stick to the road better when it is raining, too.

It is very important to take good care of your tires and your car.

Everyone needs to help
the automobile do its job.
You can help by being a
good passenger. Drivers
can help by making sure
their car is working right.
They must also obey all
the rules of the road.
These rules make driving
safer for everyone.

WORDS YOU SHOULD KNOW

axle(AX • il) — the bar on which a wheel turns

carburetor(CAR • bih • ray • ter) — the part of a gasoline engine that mixes the gasoline with air

carriage(KAIR • ij) — a passenger vehicle that has four wheels and is usually pulled by horses

combustion(kum • BUST • shun) — the process of burning

crankshaft(CRANK • shaft) — a part of the automobile engine that is connected to the piston

cylinder(SILL • in • der) — a part of the automobile engine that is shaped like a tube

dashboard(DASH • bord) — the panel below the front window and behind the steering wheel in an automobile

design(dih • ZINE) — plan something especially by drawing how it should look

energy(EN • er • gee) — power to move things; work

fossil fuel(FOSS • il FYOOL) — a substance used to provide energy that comes from the remains of plants or animals that lived long ago

future(FYOO • cher) — the time that is yet to come

gear(GEER) — a wheel with teeth around the edge

inventor(in • VEN • ter) — a person who thinks up new ideas and makes new things

limousine(LIM • oh • zeen) — a large automobile

luxury(LUKSH • er • ee) — something that is expensive and not considered necessary

piston(PIST • un) — a part of the automobile engine that goes up and down in the cylinder

power(POW • er) — energy used to do work

refinery(re • FINE • er • ee) — a factory where oil is made into gasoline

solar(SOH • ler) — of or coming from the sun

tame(TAIM) — to take from a wild state and make gentle

vapor(VAY • per) — fine particles; mist, steam

INDEX

About the Author

Sylvia Wilkinson was born in Durham, North Carolina and has taught at UNC, William and Mary, Sweet Briar College and held numerous writer-in-residence posts. Her awards include a Eugene Saxton Memorial Trust, a Wallace Stegner Creative Writing Fellowship, a Mademoiselle *Merit Award for Literature, two Sir Raleigh Awards for Literature, a National Endowment for the Arts Grant, and a Guggenheim Fellow. In addition to five novels, she has written a nonfiction series on auto racing* "The World of Racing" *published by Childrens Press; and articles for* Sports Illustrated, Madem, Ingenue, True, The American Scholar, The Writer, *and others.*

Sylvia Wilkinson is head timer and scorer for Paul Newman's Can-Am racing team.